moonchild

by laura muensterer

Copyright 2020 Laura Muensterer.
Instagram: @lnmpoems
www.lauramuensterer.com

Published by Kelley Creative
www.kelleycreative.design. All rights reserved. This book or any portion thereof may not be reproduced or used in any manner whatsoever without the express written permission of the publisher, except for the use of brief quotations in a book review.

ISBNs:
978-1-7345677-4-8 Hardback
978-1-7345677-5-5 Paperback
978-1-7345677-6-2 eBook

Cover artwork by Nicole Scherer.
www.ellehell.com
The text type was set in Jomolhari.

foreword

I have been fortunate to know Laura Muensterer the majority of her life. She was an unusual and remarkable child: mature and articulate with a penchant for making wry observations about the world. While I was an adult when I met Laura, I never once felt the need to talk down to her. I was able to converse with her as one adult mind to another.

While getting to know Laura, I sensed a persistent melancholy. She could not help but ruminate over existential questions that other children would not be aware of (much less be thinking about). Her seriousness, perceptiveness, and intellectual yearning — the very qualities that impressed me — were also making her profoundly unhappy.

Laura is a deep and complicated person, and there are many routes you can take to understand her; however, there is one idea that I have returned to often: "It is better to be Socrates dissatisfied than a fool satisfied" (John Stuart Mill). As many know, Socrates was a Greek philosopher who said, "the unexamined life is not worth living." He devoted his life to asking difficult questions that many found unsettling.

In *moonchild*, you will experience first-hand the workings of a mind that was born "Socrates dissatisfied." Despite the pain Laura's complicated mind brings her, it holds great worth and beauty. As Mill states: "A highly-endowed being will always feel that any happiness which he can look for… is imperfect. But he can learn to bear its imperfections." This is ultimately what *moonchild* is about. It's Laura's nature to question and examine everything. While it can make her unhappy, it does not mean anything is wrong with her.

The book you are about to read is a brave and beautiful collection of poems written for anyone who has ever laid awake at night, contemplating the meaning of life and struggling to find their place in it. While it takes courage to reach into the darkness and grasp for answers, it takes even more courage to let people watch you do it.

— J. Michael Ambrosio

"The moon is a loyal companion. It never leaves. It's always there, watching, steadfast, knowing us in our light and dark moments, changing forever just as we do. Every day it's a different version of itself. Sometimes weak and wan, sometimes strong and full of light. The moon understands what it means to be human. Uncertain. Alone. Cratered by imperfections."

— Tahereh Mafi

moonchild

the darkness and light
live inside me
creating a universe of

thoughts
expectations
and desires

that i try my best
to balance
despite the sun's
constant absence

laura muensterer

black or white
fact or fiction

it's all the same
when you're living
in the clouds

waiting for the sun to rise
so you can finally
open your eyes
and experience
life's beautiful skies

— *moonchild*

part I

the darkness

moonchild

my emotions are fleeting
i rarely feel one thing
for very long

sometimes i wonder
if i am the moon
encased in a human body

cycling through every season
constantly waiting for my turn
to return full

— limbo

laura muensterer

no matter your words
you cannot say anything worse
than what i have already told myself

    — i am my biggest bully

moonchild

sometimes it feels like
i'm more than one person

changing roles
as if my unfiltered soul

does not deserve
to be experienced whole

— *internal conflicts*

laura muensterer

you judge me as if
i am not already
silently judging myself

    — the damage is already done

moonchild

i wish confidence was something
i could buy

instead of something
i am constantly chasing

as if it is
some sort of prize

      — i am my own competition

laura muensterer

we are so mean
to each other
as if negativity
is the answer

    — self-love is the solution

moonchild

it's a sad day
when you realize
"sorry" is more than a word

it's a symbol
for your own perceived
lack of worth

— *not every apology is necessary*

laura muensterer

voices fill my head with
self-doubt and insecurities

so i push aside
happiness and fulfillment
to give them more room

sooner than later
there will be no more space
for good things to bloom

— barren

moonchild

every time i think
i know who i am
and what i want

my feelings change
my emotions shift

and i end up
back where i started
trying to pick up
the pieces of my past

as if they hold clues to
the person i have yet
to become

— the future is unwritten

laura muensterer

my disguise is
my coping mechanism

a way for me to hide
my true feelings

and prevent
a sea of uncertainty

from flowing out
from under me

— drowning

moonchild

i often analyze myself
as if i am a puzzle
that can be solved

— mind games

laura muensterer

it's important to recognize
the difference between your past
and your beliefs about the past

       — *opinions taint facts*

moonchild

you may think
conscious consumption
is about what you eat

but in reality
it's about what you

see
hear
and read

— choose carefully

laura muensterer

if you never spend
any time alone
you'll eventually become
someone else's clone

     — *love yourself first*

moonchild

my mind races
and i try my best
to catch it

however over the years
i've learned
anxiety never gets tired

— pace yourself

laura muensterer

as you grow older
you learn how to
parent yourself

wiping away your tears
treating yourself to sweets
and finding new ways
to rationalize your fears

all of this becomes so normal
you forget self-sufficiency
is your crutch

something you use
to fill yourself up

when all you're doing
is depriving yourself
of reaching out
and asking someone else
for help

*— the dangers of being
independent*

moonchild

our world is filled
with workaholics

people running around
a hamster wheel

as if there is a race
to be won

*— there is no trophy
waiting for you*

laura muensterer

no critic is worse
than the critic who lies
within ourselves

*— not every voice is worth
listening to*

moonchild

my future self
speaks to me
she reminds me
to never give up

she reassures me
great things lie ahead
she promises me
the work will be worth it

laura muensterer

i want to believe her
and have unwavering trust
in her words

but no matter how hard i try
doubt is always waiting
around the corner

trying to convince me
that i am undeserving
of the happiness
i have worked so hard for

— *false hope*

moonchild

i am made of
love
joy
and hope

a dash of guilt
a pinch of repressed emotions
and a spoonful of unhealed trauma

— human

laura muensterer

we talk as if
there is a solution
an answer
to my suffering

— therapy

moonchild

constant guilt and self-doubt
will turn you into a person
who no longer loves herself

— consequences

laura muensterer

happiness is fleeting
i try so hard to catch it
hold on to it
and make it mine forever

— lust

moonchild

relationships are a balance
between wins and losses

sometimes
you compromise

other times
you take a vow of silence

— *the silent treatment*

laura muensterer

lies creep
into my spine

make cracks
in my bones

and remind me
no one is deserving

of being welcomed
into my home

— lessons

moonchild

i am filled
with insecurities

often positive
always curious

and simply trying
to find my place
in this world

> *— please be patient*

laura muensterer

like a candle
some days i burn so bright
you can smell success
in the air

and other times
my light starts dimming
and there is no smoke
in sight

— burnt out

moonchild

i tear myself up
ripping apart my edges
like torn pages in a book

criticizing every flaw
overanalyzing every action
never giving myself the chance
to piece myself back together

one day i hope
i find the courage
to accept myself

instead of ripping myself apart
i put myself back together
piece by piece

kissing my bruises
embracing my insecurities
and reminding myself
that everything will be all right

— baby steps

laura muensterer

for too long
i have put boundaries
around my creativity

creating rules and requirements
for expressing my artistry
as if there is a standard

and a specific set
of expectations
i must reach

— perfectionist

moonchild

every so often
my inner child makes
an appearance

she begs for acceptance
cries for forgiveness
and aches for understanding

i try to calm her chaos
with kind words
and soothing whispers

laura muensterer

but she will not give up
until i have fully listened to
her side of the story

the side that i have
pushed away countless times
as if my lack of acknowledgment
is all that is needed

to make her disappear forever
deep into my subconscious
where countless stories
await their happy ending

— cliff hanger

moonchild

one by one
seconds pass us by
like a timer counting down
our last moments

yet i still choose
to live in the future
and worry about
what has yet to happen

creating scenarios
in my head
as if i am the sole decider
of my fate

laura muensterer

the universe must laugh at me
as i scheme
plan
and contemplate every action

while the clock
hangs on the wall

waiting for me to realize
none of it matters
not at all

— wasted time

moonchild

everything in your life
is taking up space
in your mind

you only have
so many rooms for rent
ideally you will be
the only occupant

as we all know
misery loves company
and until you make peace
with this misery

it will continue to assume
your space is meant
to be shared

— unwanted tenants

laura muensterer

anxiety binds you
to assumptions
traps you
in false predictions

and constantly reminds you
of your lack of control
over the people around you

the environment you live in
and the mistakes
you have yet to make

— paranoid

moonchild

like an animal
in the jungle
hunting its next meal

i too am on a journey of
finding creative endeavors
that feed my mind

the joy
stimulation
and fuel
it desperately craves

— *hungry*

laura muensterer

my eyes deceive me
and tell me lies about my beauty
diminishing the powerful woman
i see before me

         — *she deserves more*

moonchild

criticisms cut deep
into my subconscious

planting themselves like trees
that fail to grow any leaves

they simply take up space
in my mind

while providing my insecurities
with all the air they need
to breathe

— parasites

laura muensterer

i push people away
who show me love and affection
yet welcome a world
who has turned me cold

— naivety

moonchild

my soul is a stranger
i have yet to truly know

i shake its hand
and welcome it
into my home

yet we never talk
about anything with meaning

we simply sit and stare
at one another

wondering where we lost
our connection to each other

— detached

laura muensterer

the pressure
to be beautiful

burns into
my every being

setting fire
to my insides

leaving me with a skeleton
of self-esteem

— crime scene

moonchild

when you're a nurturer
it can be hard to recognize

when your care for others
has started to replace

the care you're supposed
to give yourself

— red flag

laura muensterer

the dance
between needing and wanting
is never-ending

                — questions

moonchild

every relationship
has its foundation

beginning with a few pieces
and eventually growing
into full houses

each betrayal costs us
a piece of our dwelling

until one day
we find ourselves with no place
to call home

so we move on
and find a new person
we can trust with our secrets

— *circle of life*

laura muensterer

some days
i can feel the earth crying

not because of the damage
we have caused

but because the environment
we live in

is a reflection of
how we treat ourselves

— mirror

moonchild

my body and i
get into fights

about who is at fault
for the sicknesses
in my life

maybe one day
we'll compromise
and realize

we each have
a part to play
in my lifelong decay

— *accountability*

laura muensterer

i constantly ponder
other people's opinions
as if their views
are ever really what's true

— *delusion*

moonchild

my bruises show my courage
my scratches show my curiosity
my scars show my childhood

yet i look at myself
and judge every discoloration
as if it's an imperfection

— badges of honor

laura muensterer

we somehow believe
by restricting our pleasures
we are saving up
for even better weather

— *flawed logic*

moonchild

most of the day
i live in my head

for how often
i am there

you'd think i'd have more
than a couple of chairs

   — comfort breeds complacency

laura muensterer

on the outside
i am cool
calm
and collected

perfecting the ideal facade
so no one figures out
my most hated flaws

— *masked*

moonchild

change being constant
used to scare me
but now that i'm older

the only thing worse
than change
is my own attachment

        — everything is temporary

laura muensterer

the drive to succeed
accelerates me forward

yet around every corner
i find myself
at a standstill

questioning my motives
and whether the speed i crave
is benefiting my future

or simply allowing me
to ignore the obstacles
i have already braved

— never satisfied

moonchild

the universe asks me
where my head has been
why i never return its calls

i try to explain
i've been going through things
but the universe doesn't care
about my silly excuses

it has seen me succeed
and overcome many challenges
yet i choose to feed
into the drama around me

when i could be
taking the lead
and building my own dreams

— *missed opportunities*

laura muensterer

i used to trust
the people around me
i used to feel safe
everywhere i went

now i simply tolerate
my surroundings
knowing that in time
everything loses its security

leaving you out in the cold
looking for someone's
hand to hold

— deserted

moonchild

when you don't fit
the status quo
you shrink yourself
to survive

molding yourself to
other people's expectations
trying to find comfort
in their acceptance

when all you really do
is suffocate your soul
from ever truly feeling whole

— empty

laura muensterer

some may call
my lack of awareness
ignorant and irresponsible

what they don't realize
is my lack of knowledge
is a coping mechanism

that keeps me from spiraling
into a great depression

i will always know a little
but never too much

this is my strategy
and it has taken
good care of me

— survival method

moonchild

every year i expect
recognition for my hard work
praise for my persistence
acknowledgment of my sacrifices

every year
i end up disappointed
not in the world
but in myself

because the world
has wasted no time
in showing me its unfairness
and displaying its dark side
for all to see

yet the one who refuses
to accept these truths
time and time again
is me

— *gullible*

laura muensterer

i make the bed
do the laundry
wash the dishes

patiently waiting
for my moment
to feel something beyond
routine existence

— purgatory

moonchild

i was shouting
for years
and no one
ever heard me

years later
i realized

all the voices
had simply been
living in my head

— muted

laura muensterer

my eyes were once filled
with inspiration
complete wonder
of the world

every so often
i get a glimpse of this
former version
of myself

a girl who hadn't been damaged
and had no reason
to ever doubt herself

— muse

part II

the light

moonchild

there is a mountain
of rejections
at my feet

yet i continue
to be me

                 — i know my worth

laura muensterer

healing is not
a linear journey

but rather a mix of
ups and downs

that gradually bring you
to the clues

of why you act
the way you do

— self-discovery

moonchild

sometimes
our biggest regrets
can all be solved
with four simple words

        — it's not your fault

"what's the worst that can happen?"
she asked

"nothing"
i responded
"because i know better now"

— growth

moonchild

i laugh at people
who think
money matters

who would have thought
a simple piece of paper

would hold so much weight
in this world

    — *wealth lies within ourselves*

laura muensterer

they say smiles
are contagious
so i try my best
to spread them
everywhere i go

— optimist

moonchild

sometimes
an exit
doesn't deserve
an explanation

— you don't owe them anything

laura muensterer

whenever you refuse
to admit you're wrong
remember that
an apology is not about
being wrong at all

> *— it's about validating
> their feelings*

moonchild

our disappointments
in childhood
become our drivers
as adults

       — higher purpose

laura muensterer

once i reconnected to my spirit
soul
and higher purpose

i no longer felt like a person
wandering the world
with nowhere to call home

i am a child of the universe
and no one can ever take that
away from me

— birthright

moonchild

many people have
overlooked me
underestimated me
and viewed me
as their inferior

what they don't realize
is their lack of respect
constant judgment
and unfair treatment

anchored me to the ground
taught me to stand tall
and allowed me to become
my own competition

— thank you

laura muensterer

i do not measure
my success by
the amount of money
i have in the bank

but rather by
the risks i have taken
the losses i have overcome
and the battles i face daily

      — *every day is a milestone*

moonchild

my unconditional love
was created after experiencing pain

my unwavering optimism
was born after i got a second chance

my unbreakable heart
was built after countless rejections

*— where my strength
comes from*

laura muensterer

the beauty
of my life
is that my mess
became my message

    — silver lining

moonchild

i envy the stars
how they can be miles away
from the chaos of life
and admire everything from afar

no attachment to suffering
no expectations to be reached

they simply float about us
and silently judge our hysteria

waiting for us to realize
our most trusted example
of how to live a balanced life
has been above our heads
the whole time

— teachers

laura muensterer

i am a tree
rooted in simplicity
grounded in growth

and planted for a purpose
far beyond my own
limited perception

— *divinity*

moonchild

every "wrong" turn i have made
has led me to
an even more beautiful destination

                 — don't give up

laura muensterer

it's never been about
fame
success
or money

for none of these things
can fill you up
quite like your own
inner peace can

> *— happiness comes
from within*

moonchild

the irony of life is that
your worst moments become
your biggest milestones

— growth stems from pain

laura muensterer

the voices in our heads
are like radio stations
you get to choose
which ones you tune in to

                — the secret to sanity

moonchild

waves crash
beneath my feet

while thoughts of floating
off to sea

with no plan or direction
wash over me

— *wanderlust*

laura muensterer

what we say to ourselves
has a lot more power
than what people say about us

      — *be your own advocate*

moonchild

just like trees shed their leaves
and the moon moves
through its phases
i am evolving individual

stripping myself of what's familiar
going outside my comfort zone
and creating new identities
for myself

to test my truths
and see if what i believe
is actually what i see

— *curiosity*

laura muensterer

you may pay my salary
and provide me with
insurance benefits

a 401k
and free lunch
every weekday

but you cannot
put your name on

the insight
wisdom
and knowledge
i have worked so hard
to gain

— a note to my employer

moonchild

i forgive myself
for my lack of good judgment

for these decisions
are the reason i now know

the difference between
healthy drive
and harmful attachment

           — important distinctions

laura muensterer

failure is no longer
something i am afraid of

but rather a friend
who pushes me to go beyond
my limiting beliefs

so i face the potential i have
ignored and abandoned
time and time again

as if i have an eternity
to make a name for myself

       — *every minute matters*

moonchild

i inhale the earth around me
sip on the serenity
of life's simplicity

and gather
treasured memories
in my hands

as the wind carries me
through new seasons
of growth

— blessings

laura muensterer

there are people who give up
lose hope
and find negativity
in everything

and then
there are people
like you and i

people who have experienced
pain
sadness
and betrayal

and choose to be
a light in people's life
anyway

*— where my hope
comes from*

moonchild

my journey to wholeness
involved learning that
to be complete
i must first accept me

— *foundation*

laura muensterer

i am learning every day
there is nothing wrong with me

we are all imperfect
in our own special way

this is not our downfall
but rather our saving grace

for if we were all problem-free
it would be hard to see past
the facade that is "me"

— divinely designed

moonchild

when music plays
i escape my mind
for a few minutes

and take time to appreciate
the art of expressing myself
through a different medium

one with more depth
than our words
can ever carry

— medicine

laura muensterer

there is a world of
possibilities at my feet

encasing my eyes with wonder
dilating my pupils
with my wildest dreams

filling my lungs with
oxygen so smooth

i feel like i have been
completely renewed

    — *anything is possible*

moonchild

i live between two worlds
one of fact
one of fiction

attempting to create
a concise narrative
out of internal chaos

trying to connect the pieces
of my past
present
and desired future

when the only true solution
is to simply allow my mind
to be free
just as it was meant to be

— remedy

laura muensterer

whenever you're in a rut
remind yourself

trees grow
flowers bloom

clouds disappear
the sun shines

and the day starts over
just as it did yesterday

— nothing lasts forever

moonchild

i am hungry
not for food
but for a life
that's innately mine

— *creator*

laura muensterer

no one is in your body
no one has peeked
into your mind

remember this
when they try
to convince you

they know your struggles
better than you do

— you hold the solution

moonchild

the beauty of selfishness
is that it is the first step
to selflessness

— unexpected benefits

laura muensterer

if you look
inside yourself
you'll discover

more gardens
more flowers
more beauty

than what you could
ever find next door

      — you are a masterpiece

moonchild

before you pour yourself
into your next project
considering watering

your own mind
body
and soul first

— note to self

laura muensterer

just like the sun
welcomes us
in the morning

i too will rise taller
brighter
and more powerful
than before

— rebirth

moonchild

my wealth is measured by
the hearts i touch
the people i embrace
and the love i share daily

— abundance

a note from the author

Dear friend,

As you read this, I am relishing in the beauty of connecting with you and serving as a small — but hopefully significant — part of your spiritual journey. I hope this book has put you on a path of alignment, where your innermost dreams and desires can be brought to light.

Thank you for allowing me to share myself with you and connect with your soul. Your journey is just now beginning, and it will be more beautiful than you could ever imagine.

XOXO
Laura

about the author

Laura Muensterer is an avid writer who uses creative storytelling to express her innermost thoughts, emotions, and fears about the world. Through poetry and illustration, Laura explores various aspects of the human experience while shedding light on the many ways our past shapes our present and future self.

After earning a B.A. in public relations and a minor in psychology, Laura became an advertising copywriter, writing for clients like AT&T and Citibank. During this time, she self-published her first book, *freebird* (later republished under Kelley Creative). Shortly after, Laura became a Certified Life Coach and began working on her second poetry collection, *moonchild*.

Born in Munich, Germany, Laura lived in Dallas, Texas for fifteen years before moving to San Diego, California. A true Texan, she loves to ride horses and enjoy the simpler things in life. When she's not writing or coaching, you can find Laura spoiling her four pets, Beau, Bella, Luna, and Nova. You can follow her writing journey at @lnmpoems on Instagram.

www.ingramcontent.com/pod-product-compliance
Lightning Source LLC
Chambersburg PA
CBHW071359080526
44587CB00017B/3131